Awesome Ancient Animals

Huge Hunters Roam the Earth

Ancient Mammals

Dougal Dixon

An Hachette Company

First published in the United States by
New Forest Press, an imprint of Octopus Publishing Group Ltd

www.octopusbook.usa.com

Copyright © Octopus Publishing Group Ltd 2012

Published by arrangement with Black Rabbit Books

PO Box 784, Mankato, MN 56002

Dixon, Dougal.
Huge Hunters Roam the Earth : Ancient Mammals / by Dougal Dixon.
p. cm. -- (Awesome Ancient Animals)
Summary: "Describes the animals of the Tertiary Period, when
huge open plains of grass formed, and mammals developed long
legs to suit this new environment. Includes an Animal Families
glossary, prehistory timeline, and pronunciation guides"-- Provided
by publisher.
Includes index.
ISBN 978-1-84898-624-4 (hardcover, library bound)
1. Paleontology--Tertiary--Juvenile literature. 2. Animals, Fossil--
Juvenile literature. I. Title.
QE736.D588 2013
560'.178--dc23
2012002742

Printed and bound in the USA

16 15 14 13 12 1 2 3 4 5

Publisher: Tim Cook Editor: Margaret Parrish Designer: Steve West

Contents

Introduction

This map shows how the Earth looked at the end of the Tertiary Period. As the continents moved, the landscape changed, and new animals evolved.

This map shows how the Earth looks today. See how different it is! The continents have split up and moved around.

Awesome Ancient Animals follows the evolution of animals.

Earth's history is divided into eras, which are divided into periods. These last millions of years. *Huge Hunters Roam the Earth* takes you back to the Tertiary Period. During this time, great open plains of grass formed. Mammals from this time developed long legs to suit this new environment.

A LOOK BACK IN TIME

This timeline shows how simple creatures evolved into many differnt and complex life-forms. This took millions and millions of years. In the chart, MYA stands for million years ago.

	BOOK	PERIOD	
CENOZOIC ERA	**THE ICE AGE**	1.81 MYA to now QUATERNARY	This is a time of Ice Ages and mammals. Our direct relatives, Homo sapiens, appear.
	ANCIENT MAMMALS	65 to 1.81 MYA TERTIARY	Giant mammals and huge, hunting birds rule. Our first human relatives start to evolve.
MESOZOIC ERA	**CRETACEOUS LIFE**	145 to 65 MYA CRETACEOUS	Huge dinosaurs evolve. They die out by the end of this period.
	JURASSIC LIFE	200 to 145 MYA JURASSIC	Large and small dinosaurs and flying creatures develop.
	TRIASSIC LIFE	250 to 200 MYA TRIASSIC	The "Age of Dinosaurs" begins. Early mammals live alongside them.
PALEOZOIC ERA	**EARLY LIFE**	299 to 250 MYA PERMIAN	Sail-backed reptiles start to appear.
		359 to 299 MYA CARBONIFEROUS	The first reptiles appear and tropical forests develop.
		416 to 359 MYA DEVONIAN	Bony fish evolve. Trees and insects come on the scene.
		444 to 416 MYA SILURIAN	Fish with jaws develop and sea animals start living on land.
		488 to 444 MYA ORDOVICIAN	Primitive fish, trilobites, shellfish, and plants evolve.
		542 to 488 MYA CAMBRIAN	First animals with skeletons appear.

Megistotherium

Before modern carnivores such as lions and bears appeared, a group of predators called creodonts roamed the Earth. *Megistotherium* was the biggest, with a skull twice as long as a tiger's. It is probably the largest hunting land mammal of all time.

With a head 4 ft (1.2 m) long and a body the size of a bison, *Megistotherium* was big and powerful enough to hunt elephants!

Not all creodonts were huge—some were as small as a weasel. But all of them were fierce hunters. They had bone-crushing, meat-ripping teeth, as this skull of a creodont shows.

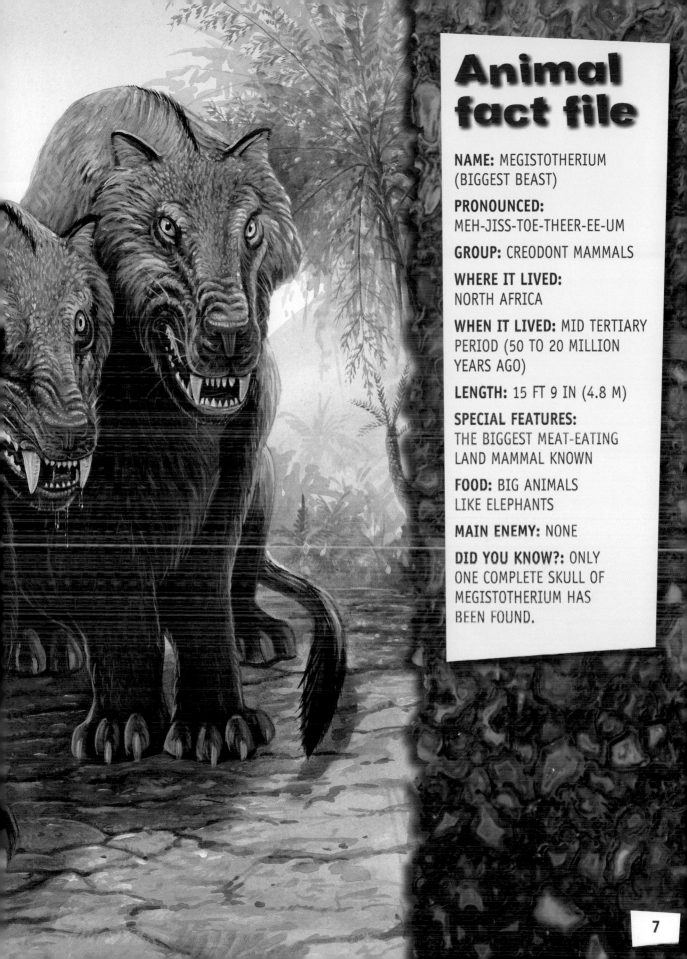

Animal fact file

NAME: MEGISTOTHERIUM (BIGGEST BEAST)

PRONOUNCED: MEH-JISS-TOE-THEER-EE-UM

GROUP: CREODONT MAMMALS

WHERE IT LIVED: NORTH AFRICA

WHEN IT LIVED: MID TERTIARY PERIOD (50 TO 20 MILLION YEARS AGO)

LENGTH: 15 FT 9 IN (4.8 M)

SPECIAL FEATURES: THE BIGGEST MEAT-EATING LAND MAMMAL KNOWN

FOOD: BIG ANIMALS LIKE ELEPHANTS

MAIN ENEMY: NONE

DID YOU KNOW?: ONLY ONE COMPLETE SKULL OF MEGISTOTHERIUM HAS BEEN FOUND.

Moropus

Scientists can tell how an animal lived by looking at its skeleton. The head of *Moropus* was like that of a horse, which shows that it was a plant-eater. Its front legs were longer than its hind legs. It could stretch its neck upward to feed from high tree branches. Modern-day giraffes are built the same way.

The skeleton of *Moropus* looks like the skeleton of a horse. In fact, the two are close relatives, although Moropus had claws instead of hooves.

Moropus used its big claws to pull down branches and reach leaves that grew in the treetops. It was the biggest member of the chalicothere group.

Animal fact file

NAME: MOROPUS (SLOW FOOT)

PRONOUNCED: MOOR-OH-PUS

GROUP: CHALICOTHERE FAMILY OF PERISSODACTYLS

WHERE IT LIVED: NORTH AMERICA

WHEN IT LIVED: MID TO LATE TERTIARY PERIOD (23 TO 14 MILLION YEARS AGO)

HEIGHT: 8 FT (2.4 M) AT THE SHOULDER

SPECIAL FEATURES: BIG CLAWS FOR RIPPING DOWN VEGETATION

FOOD: LEAVES

MAIN ENEMY: BIG MEAT-EATING MAMMALS LIKE AMPHICYON

DID YOU KNOW?: WHEN PALEONTOLOGISTS FIRST FOUND THE MOROPUS'S CLAWS, THEY THOUGHT THEY CAME FROM A GIANT SLOTH.

Pyrotherium

In the Tertiary Period, South America and North America were far apart. Different mammals evolved in South America and some looked like those that lived on other continents, although they were not related. *Pyrotherium* looked like an elephant.

Male *Pyrotherium* may have used their tusks and trunks in fights over females.

Pyrotherium probably lived like an elephant does, digging in the ground with its tusks and picking up food with its trunk.

Animal fact file

NAME: PYROTHERIUM (FIRE MAMMAL, BECAUSE ITS FOSSILS WERE FOUND NEAR A VOLCANO)

PRONOUNCED: PI-RO-THEER-EE-UM

GROUP: PYROTHERE GROUP OF THE XENUNGULATES, WHICH MEANS "FOREIGN-HOOFED MAMMALS"

WHERE IT LIVED: BOLIVIA AND ARGENTINA

WHEN IT LIVED: MID TERTIARY PERIOD (29 TO 23 MILLION YEARS AGO)

LENGTH: 9 FT (2.7 M)

SPECIAL FEATURES: TRUNK AND TUSKS

FOOD: PLANTS

MAIN ENEMY: BIG MEAT-EATING MARSUPIALS

DID YOU KNOW?: PYROTHERIUM HAD THE TUSKS AND TRUNK OF AN ELEPHANT, TEETH LIKE A HIPPOPOTAMUS AND THE EAR BONES OF A HOOFED MAMMAL. IT IS DIFFICULT TO DETERMINE WHO ITS MODERN RELATIVES ARE.

Uintatherium

The *Uintatherium* had a big heavy body and horns like a rhinoceros, but the two are not related. Many rhinoceros-like mammals lived in the early Tertiary Period. They probably evolved to replace horned dinosaurs like *Triceratops*, which had become extinct.

Uintatherium weighed about two tons and supported itself on massive, stumpy legs. It is likely that only the males had long, spiked tusks, which they used for defense.

Its six horns and sharp tusks must have made *Uintatherium* look frightening. However, it was a gentle plant-eater.

Animal fact file

NAME: UINTATHERIUM (MAMMAL FROM THE UINTA MOUNTAINS IN UTAH)

PRONOUNCED: YOU-IN-TA-THEER-EE-UM

GROUP: UINTATHERES

WHERE IT LIVED: UTAH

WHEN IT LIVED: EARLY TERTIARY PERIOD (40 TO 35 MILLION YEARS AGO)

LENGTH: 13 FT (4 M)

SPECIAL FEATURES: THREE PAIRS OF HORNS AND A PAIR OF SHARP TUSKS

FOOD: PLANTS

MAIN ENEMY: NONE

DID YOU KNOW?: IN THE 1870S TWO AMERICAN PALEONTOLOGISTS, OTHNIEL MARSH AND EDWARD COPE, ARGUED OVER WHO SHOULD NAME THIS ANIMAL. IT WAS FINALLY NAMED UINTATHERIUM BY ANOTHER PALEONTOLOGIST, JOSEPH LEIDY, IN 1872.

Megacerops

The brontotheres were rhinoceros-shaped mammals that lived in the early Tertiary Period. They ranged in size from little animals no bigger than a rabbit to huge beasts like *Megacerops*, which weighed more than an elephant.

Despite its big skull, *Megacerops* had a small brain. Most dinosaurs had bigger brains in relation to their size.

The horns of *Megacerops* and the other brontotheres were not true horns. They were bony lumps covered by skin, like giraffe horns.

Animal fact file

NAME: MEGACEROPS (BIG HORNED FACE)

PRONOUNCED: MEG-AH-SAIR-OPS

GROUP: BRONTOTHERES (THUNDER MAMMALS)

WHERE IT LIVED: WESTERN NORTH AMERICA

WHEN IT LIVED: EARLY TERTIARY PERIOD (58 TO 30 MILLION YEARS AGO)

LENGTH: 13 FT (4 M) LONG AND 8 FT (2.4 M) HIGH AT THE SHOULDER

SPECIAL FEATURES: MASSIVE Y-SHAPED NOSE DECORATION

FOOD: LOW-GROWING VEGETATION

MAIN ENEMY: BIG MEAT-EATING MAMMALS SUCH AS CREODONTS

DID YOU KNOW?: SCIENTISTS THINK THAT ONLY MALES HAD A NOSE DECORATION, WHICH WAS USED TO ATTRACT FEMALES. THEY PROBABLY LIVED IN HERDS.

Indricotherium

This massive beast is another ancient relative of the rhinoceros, although it did not have a nose horn. An animal this size would not have needed a weapon to defend itself. It is the biggest land mammal ever to have lived.

Indricotherium had two pairs of teeth at the front of its mouth. It also had two tusklike teeth on the upper jaw and two on the lower jaw. These were used for scraping leaves from branches.

Indricotherium lived like a giraffe. Its long legs, on three-toed feet, held its body high above the ground. The 3-ft- (1-m-) long neck and head allowed it to reach the tops of the highest trees.

Animal fact file

NAME: INDRICOTHERIUM (MAMMAL OF INDRIK—A MONSTER OF LOCAL LEGENDS)

PRONOUNCED: IN-DRIK-OH-THEER-EE-UM

GROUP: PERISSODACTYLS (ODD-TOED HOOFED MAMMALS)

WHERE IT LIVED: PAKISTAN

WHEN IT LIVED: MID TERTIARY PERIOD (20 TO 30 MILLION YEARS AGO)

LENGTH: 26 FT (8 M) LONG AND 15 FT (4.5 M) TALL AT THE SHOULDER. AN ELEPHANT IS ABOUT 23 FT (7 M) LONG AND 10 FT (3 M) TALL AT THE SHOULDER

SPECIAL FEATURES: ENORMOUS SIZE

FOOD: LEAVES AND TWIGS

MAIN ENEMY: NONE

DID YOU KNOW?: INDRICOTHERIUM WEIGHED ABOUT 11 TONS (10 METRIC TONS).

Basilosaurus

Basilosaurus was one of the earliest whales. Like all whales, it was a mammal. Although mammals evolved on land, many of them returned to the sea at the beginning of the Tertiary Period, probably to escape vicious predators or to look for new food sources.

Like modern whales, *Basilosaurus* had to come to the surface to breathe. It had nostrils that functioned like the blowhole on top of a whale's head.

Animal fact file

NAME: BASILOSAURUS
(KING LIZARD)

PRONOUNCED:
BASS-IL-OH-SORE-US

GROUP: ARCHAEOCETE WHALES

WHERE IT LIVED: ALL THE OCEANS

WHEN IT LIVED: EARLY TERTIARY PERIOD (45 TO 35 MILLION YEARS AGO)

LENGTH: 59 FT (18 M)

SPECIAL FEATURES: A LONG, THIN AND FLEXIBLE BODY, IDEAL FOR CATCHING FISH

FOOD: FISH AND CEPHALOPODS

MAIN ENEMY: MAYBE SHARKS

DID YOU KNOW?:
BASILOSAURUS HAS A NAME LIKE A DINOSAUR BECAUSE THE SCIENTIST WHO FOUND ITS FOSSILS THOUGHT THEY CAME FROM A GIANT REPTILE.

This fossil shows the long, snakelike backbone of *Basilosaurus*. In 1845, fossil-collector Albert Koch put together bones from several skeletons and exhibited his "giant sea serpent."

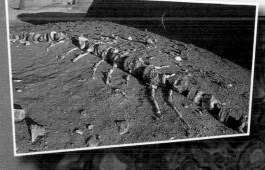

Desmostylus

This hippopotamus-like animal with strange crooked legs lived near the Pacific Ocean in the Tertiary Period. It probably used its tusks and heavy teeth to dig for shellfish on the seabed, or it may have grazed on seaweed. Scientists are not really sure what it ate!

Its inward-turning feet made *Desmostylus* clumsy on land. In water, however, it was graceful. It walked across the seabed like a hippopotamus does today.

This is a fossil of a *Desmostylus* tooth. From the chemicals in its teeth and bones, scientists know that it spent most of its time in water.

Animal fact file

NAME: DESMOSTYLUS (CHAIN-TOOTH, AFTER THE WAY THE BACK TEETH LINK TOGETHER)

PRONOUNCED: DES-MO-STY-LUS

GROUP: DESMOSTYLID MAMMALS

WHERE IT LIVED: COASTS OF JAPAN AND CALIFORNIA

WHEN IT LIVED: MID TO LATE TERTIARY PERIOD (14 TO 19 MILLION YEARS AGO)

LENGTH: 6 FT (1.8 M)

SPECIAL FEATURES: LUMBERING GAIT AND POWERFUL TEETH

FOOD: SHELLFISH OR SEAWEED

MAIN ENEMY: SHARKS

DID YOU KNOW?: THE NEAREST LIVING RELATIVE OF DESMOSTYLUS IS THE ELEPHANT.

Gomphotherium

Animals of the Tertiary Period that resembed elephants started as small piglike animals. They soon developed into big beasts with tusks and trunks. *Gomphotherium* had four tusks—two on the upper jaw and two on the lower jaw.

The shovel-like tusks on the lower jaw were used to dig for food on the forest floor and at the bottom of streams and lakes.

It is not certain that *Gomphotherium* had a trunk. Trunks are made of flesh, which does not fossilize. However, its neck was too short for its head to reach the ground, and the skull shows features similar to the trunk area of modern elephants. Scientists think *Gomphotherium* had a trunk.

Animal fact file

NAME: GOMPHOTHERIUM (BOLTED MAMMAL)

PRONOUNCED: GOM-FO-THEER-EE-UM

GROUP: ELEPHANTS

WHERE IT LIVED: EUROPE, KENYA, PAKISTAN, JAPAN, AND NORTH AMERICA

WHEN IT LIVED: LATE TERTIARY PERIOD (23 TO 3 MILLION YEARS AGO)

LENGTH: 13 FT (4 M)

SPECIAL FEATURES: ELEPHANT WITH A PAIR OF TUSKS ON THE UPPER JAW AND ANOTHER ON THE LOWER

FOOD: PLANTS

MAIN ENEMY: NONE

DID YOU KNOW?: GOMPHOTHERIUM PROBABLY EVOLVED IN AFRICA AND THEN SPREAD TO THE REST OF THE WORLD.

Deinotherium

Modern elephants have their tusks on the upper jaw. *Deinotherium* had its tusks on the lower jaw, and they turned downward. These tusks would have been used as picks for digging up roots and other ground vegetation.

Deinotherium is the second biggest land animal known, after Indricotherium. It existed for almost 20 million years.

The discovery of *Deinotherium* skulls in Greece may have led to the legend of the Cyclops—the one-eyed giant. The nostrils in the skull are fused into a single hole, which looks like an enormous eye socket.

Animal fact file

NAME: DEINOTHERIUM (TERRIBLE MAMMAL)

PRONOUNCED: DY-NO-THEER-EE-UM

GROUP: ELEPHANTS

WHERE IT LIVED: AFRICA AND SOUTHERN EUROPE

WHEN IT LIVED: LATE TERTIARY PERIOD (20 TO 2 MILLION YEARS AGO)

HEIGHT: 13 FT (4 M) AT THE SHOULDERS

SPECIAL FEATURES: DOWNWARD-CURVING TUSKS ON THE LOWER JAW

FOOD: PLANTS

MAIN ENEMY: NONE

DID YOU KNOW?: DEINOTHERIUM LIVED AT THE SAME TIME AS OUR EARLIEST HUMAN ANCESTORS.

Sivatherium

Sivatherium had horns and looked like a moose, but it was really a kind of giraffe. It was not the long-necked, long-legged animal that we know today, but a heavily built browsing animal. It probably had a muscular upper lip, like the long nose of a moose.

Only two types of giraffe exist today—the long-necked giraffe of the African plains and the short-necked okapi of the forests. In the Tertiary Period there were dozens of different giraffes.

Sivatherium had two pairs of horns, but only the back pair were like antlers. The pair at the front were very small.

Animal fact file

NAME: SIVATHERIUM (MAMMAL OF SHIVA—AN INDIAN GOD)

PRONOUNCED: SEE-VA-THEER-EE-UM

GROUP: GIRAFFES

WHERE IT LIVED: AFRICA AND ASIA

WHEN IT LIVED: LATE TERTIARY PERIOD TO THE EARLY QUATERNARY PERIOD (5 TO 1 MILLION YEARS AGO)

HEIGHT: 6 FT 6 IN (2 M) AT THE SHOULDER

SPECIAL FEATURES: TWO PAIRS OF HORNS

FOOD: PLANTS

MAIN ENEMY: LIONS AND GIANT BEARS

DID YOU KNOW?: ROCK PAINTINGS OF AN ANIMAL THAT LOOKS LIKE SIVATHERIUM WERE FOUND IN THE SAHARA DESERT. IT MUST HAVE SURVIVED LONG ENOUGH FOR EARLY PEOPLE TO PAINT IT.

Amphicyon

Amphicyon was as big as a grizzly bear. It was one of the largest hunting animals in the mid Tertiary Period. With its massive body and powerful legs, it would have been able to hunt most animals. It killed with its sharp, doglike teeth.

Amphicyon had short legs and walked on flat feet. It could not have run quickly and probably ambushed its prey.

The *Amphicyon* is neither a bear nor a dog, but something in between. Amphicyonids ranged from the size of a badger to the size of the biggest bears.

Animal fact file

NAME: AMPHICYON (NEARLY A DOG)

PRONOUNCED: AM-FEE-SY-ON

GROUP: AMPHICYONIDS—THE BEAR DOGS

WHERE IT LIVED: EUROPE AND NORTH AMERICA

WHEN IT LIVED: MID TERTIARY PERIOD (30 TO 14 MILLION YEARS AGO)

HEIGHT: 3 FT (1 M)

SPECIAL FEATURES: SKELETON LIKE A BEAR, TEETH OF A DOG

FOOD: OTHER ANIMALS, PARTICULARLY THE SMALL HORSES OF THE TIME

MAIN ENEMY: NONE

DID YOU KNOW?: THE BEAR-DOGS TOOK OVER FROM THE CREODONTS IN THE EARLY TERTIARY PERIOD. THEY WERE REPLACED BY THE CANIDS (WOLVES, FOXES, AND DOGS).

Animal Families Glossary

Amphicyonids—the bear-dogs. These were meat-eating mammals from the Late Tertiary Period that were related both to the bear and the dog.

Archaeocetes—the earliest group of completely marine whales. They differed from modern whales and porpoises by having teeth of different shapes and sizes, with pointed snatching teeth at the front and meat-shearing teeth at the back.

Brontotheres—a group of rhinoceros-like perissodactyls from the Early Tertiary Period. Some were the size of a pig and others as large as an elephant.

Chalicotheres—a perissodactyl group related to the horse. Instead of hooves they had claws that would have been used for tearing down branches.

Creodonts—a group of early meat-eating mammals from the Early Tertiary. Although they resembled modern wolves, weasels, and bears, they were not related to them.

Desmostylids—a group of semiaquatic mammals that lived around the Pacific Ocean in the Mid to Late Tertiary Period. They probably fed on seaweed and shellfish.

Perissodactyls—the group of odd-toed hoofed mammals. Modern forms include the horse, the rhinoceros, and the tapir. They normally have either one toe or three on the foot. The other hoofed mammal group is the artiodactyls—the even-toed hoofed mammals, and these include the sheep, the goats, and the deer.

Pyrotheres—a group of xenungulates that resembled the modern elephant, although they were not closely related to elephants. They lived in South America.

Uintatheres—a group of heavy, rhinoceros-like mammals from the Early Tertiary Period. They had several pairs of hornlike structures on their heads and a pair of long tusks.

Xenungulates—a group of hoofed mammals that lived in South America during the Tertiary Period. They were not related to the hoofed mammals of the rest of the world, but evolved independently.

Glossary

Adapted—changed to survive in a particular habitat or weather conditions.

Ambushing—lying in wait, out of sight, and then making a surprise attack.

Blowhole—a hole at the top of a whale's head that is its nostril. To breathe a whale comes to the surface of the water and blows air out of the hole and breathes air in. When the whale is under water, a flap of skin covers the hole.

Browsing—feeding on grass or leaves.

Continent—one of the world's main land masses, such as Africa and Europe.

Evolution—changes or developments that happen to all forms of life over millions of years, as a result of changes in the environment.

Evolve—to change or develop.

Extinct—animal group that no longer exists.

Fossil—the remains of a prehistoric plant or animal that has been turned to rock.

Fossilize—to turn into a fossil.

Mammal—a warm-blooded animal that is covered in hair. The female gives birth to live young and produces milk from her own body to feed them.

Marsupial—an animal, such as a kangaroo, that has a pouch on the front of its body in which it carries its young.

Moose—a type of deer from North America.

Paleontologist—a scientist who studies fossils.

Prehistory—the time before humans evolved.

Primitive—a very early stage in the development of a species.

Reptile—a cold-blooded, crawling, or creeping animals with a backbone.

Rock painting—a drawing made by our early ancestors millions of years ago.

Semiaquatic—animals that spend a lot of time in water but which need air to breathe, for example, turtles, otters, and frogs.

Sloth—a very slow-moving animal that lives in rainforests.

Tropical—a hot, wet climate found in places that are close to the equator.

Tusk—a long pointed tooth that grows outside of an animal's mouth.

Index

Picture credits

Main image: 6-7, 10-11, 16-17, 20-21 Simon Mendez; 18-19 Luis Rey;
8-9, 12-13, 14-15, 22-23, 24-25, 26-27, 28-29 Chris Tomlin 4TL, 4TR, 5 (Cenozoic
Era), 6, 8, 15, 19, 20, 23, 25 Ticktock Media archive; 5 (Mesozoic Era top, Paleozoic
Era top) Simon Mendez; 5 (Mesozoic Era center, Paleozoic Era bottom) Luis Rey; 5
(Mesozoic Era bottom) Lisa Alderson; 11 Amherst College Museum of Natural History;
27, 29 Shutterstock; 13 The Natural History Museum, London; 16 Ria Novosti/Science
Photo Library